About Almabase

Almabase is a full-fledged alumni relations software that empowers you to create an online community for alumni to network with each other for career advice and professional help, communicate with alumni, provide mentorship opportunities for students, manage online giving and alumni events.

Headquartered in San Francisco, CA Almabase works with more than 100 partner schools across the world. For more information, visit www.almabase.com

Proud partners of

Almabase, the Almabase logo, are trademarks of Almbase, Inc. All other trademarks are the property of their respective owners.

#STAY RELEVANT
INTRODUCTION

In the United States, alumni associations are almost as old as their alma maters. At the start, most of the associations were entirely voluntary, supported solely by individual alumni. Volunteers maintained mailing lists, collected dues to support activities, produced publications, and, organized events and annual meetings. alumni were the institution's first fundraisers. Development has its roots in alumni relations. The origins of the annual fund and capital campaigns are also alumni based.

Here we are now, after two centuries of hard work and building thousands of thriving alumni communities across the country. The world of alumni relations has come a long way since its inception in the early eighteenth-century. They have become a vital part of most educational institutions now thanks to the efforts of many outstanding professionals in the field. Alumni Relations professionals must have a skill set that is both broad and deep. They must be visionaries who also understand the importance of attention to detail.

With the internet revolution, the world has come online and so have alumni communities. Alumni Relations too has taken some interesting new directions over the last decade.

Further, we are going to discuss a few of these trends and how they are shaping alumni engagement experiences. We will also provide some best-practices from various institutions across the country who are doing a great job in various fields.

Finally, we would love to thank all of our 100+ partner schools for letting us into their fascinating world and for leaving us in awe of their sheer brilliance and hard-work.

We hope that you find the insights we have gathered from the experiences of our partner schools and numerous other surveys insightful!

#STAY RELEVANT

Contents

Introduction

Part One : Obligation Vs Value

Part Two : Millennials and their impact

Part Three : Digital is now default - Go online

Part Four : Dedicated Alumni Management Platforms

Part Five : Online Giving

Part Six : Data driven decisions win!

Part Seven : Communication is a two way street!

Part Eight : Budgeting blues

Part Nine : Insights into the World of Alumni Relations

Conclusion

About the guide

PART ONE
OBLIGATION VS VALUE

PART ONE : OBLIGATION VS VALUE
WHAT MOTIVATES DONORS TO GIVE?

The world around your alumni has changed. We now live in a world of value-based relationships. Don't take our word for it; take a look around and observe all the various products and services they use every day. From Amazon's customer obsession to Apple's passion for design beauty, the world has shifted from obligatory decisions to value-based relationships.

In our world of alumni relations, there are a few important factors that traditionally makes the alumni come back to them institution and give back. Some of them are:

1. They are supposed to give back - Traditional Obligation

2. Their school needs them now - Sense of Helping

3. Best place to meet their fellow alumni - Networking

Over the years a lot of players emerged in this donor market and are competing for the attention of your alumni. More than a million non-profits are vying for your alumni's support and they are better equipped to get their attention for their cause. Social media has made the process of networking available at their fingertips. With the increasing education loan debts, prices and unemployment, the traditional obligation of giving is slowly fading alive.

Along the very same lines, there is an interesting trend that evolved over the last decade and a half that changed the way alumni see their institutions for better. It is the beginning of an exciting and new landscape in the world of alumni relations.

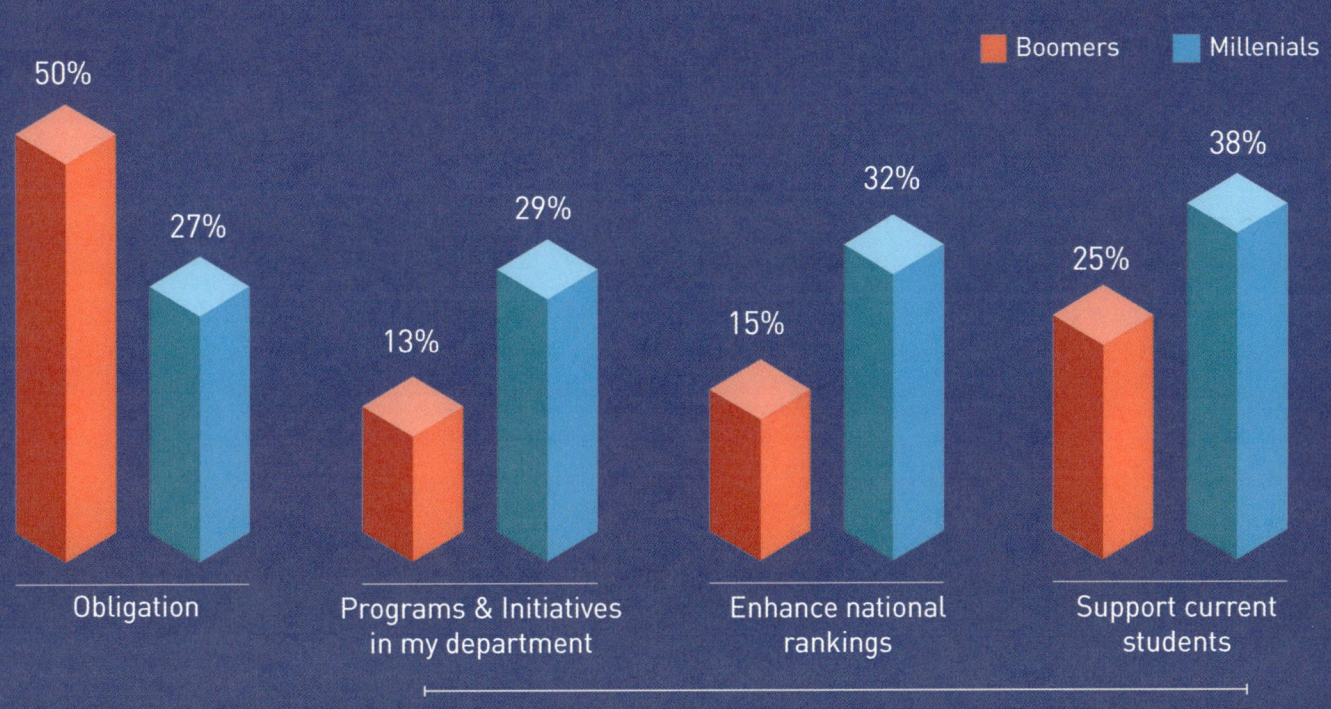

PART ONE : OBLIGATION VS VALUE
EVERY INDUSTRY IS CHANGING

Change is an inevitable phenomenon around the globe with every industry.

What's stopping alumni relations from adapting to this change?
We made some interesting observations from various studies and our own experiences.

1. Schools don't know how to reach all of their alumni

Only 20.3% of the schools have updated data of their alumni.-[1]

2. Schools don't know what their alumni want

50% of alumni discontinued their membership because they couldn't see an ROI or sufficient value.-[1]

3. Schools don't know whom or when to ask

43% of alumni haven't volunteered or helped because they are not asked to do so.-[2]

While these are big challenges, this is also a huge opportunity for your organization to embrace change. The generation for causes - the Millennials - will represent a solid 75% of the American workforce by 2025. This spirited, pro-change generation is all for supporting a cause, helping other people and eventually becoming a part of a community that's equally eager to 'make a difference'. This is a great opportunity for schools to show their alumni how their support can bring about the significant changes that they are passionate about.

PART ONE : OBLIGATION VS VALUE

" ..donors are giving as a result of the long-term relationship they have with their institutions"

- CASE President

50% of alumni discontinued their membership because they couldn't see an ROI or sufficient value.

- VAESE Alumni Relations Benchmarking Study (2016)

PART TWO

MILLENIALS AND THEIR IMPACT

PART TWO : MILLENIALS AND THEIR IMPACT
THEY ARE THE FIRST DIGITAL NATIVES

With the advent of 'Millennials', alumni engagement has taken a giant leap forward. They are the first digital natives, they are social and they are the largest generation in the history. Their affinity for technology shapes their thinking. The good news is that the technology has never been more available than it is now. All it takes is using the right tools at the right time to win them over. That said, technology should not overshadow the good old traditions that keep relationships alive.

A healthy mix of technology and tradition is the best way to keep your millennials engaged.

Millennials are also changing the landscape of giving back to the world. Unlike the generations before them, they do not incorporate giving into their lives through a sense of duty or obligation. Millennials are seeking to impact the world with not only their money, but also with their time, their talent, and their influence via social networks.

Here a few reasons why millennials are different from their previous generations!

PART TWO : MILLENIALS AND THEIR IMPACT
VALUE BASED VS OBLIGATORY GIVING

With more than a million non-profits eyeing for the Millennials' support towards their meaningful initiatives, it is indeed a challenging time for educational institutions to win the support of their younger alumni.

The reason for this is pretty straightforward: Millennials are value-based. They are less interested in donating to their alma mater, as they may not really see the same value as getting involved with an organization or another non-profit. Therefore, any school that asks for a Millennial's financial support for an unspecified cause with an unspecified impact is going to fall short of winning those gifts more often than not.

PART TWO : MILLENIALS AND THEIR IMPACT

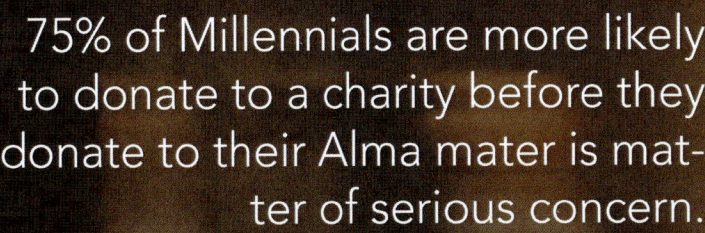

75% of Millennials are more likely to donate to a charity before they donate to their Alma mater is matter of serious concern.

Source: Millennial Alumni Report - The Chronicle of Philanthropy (2014)

PART TWO : MILLENIALS AND THEIR IMPACT
TIME, TALENT AND TREASURE

Giving for millennials has a different meaning today. Young alumni want to invest beyond their money and also devote their time and talent to widen their networks.

Having said that, we know how crucial these donations are for educational institutions to adhere to their standards of quality in education. The silver lining is that more that 73% of them are ready to give back to their Alma Mater. Give them opportunities to give back on their own terms and they are more likely to participate and give back. An alum who has given his or her time or talent in any form is far more likely to give a financial gift in the future than otherwise.

Millennial alumni with strong, long-term relationships with their schools are more likely to:

– be willing to act as fundraisers

– make a personal donation to that nonprofit

– give larger gifts than non-volunteers

– encourage friends and family to give and volunteer as well

PART TWO : MILLENIALS AND THEIR IMPACT

86% of them would love to would enjoy using their specific skills, talents, or expertise to volunteer

Source: Millennial Alumni Report - The Chronicle of Philanthropy (2014)

PART TWO : MILLENIALS AND THEIR IMPACT
MAKE IT PERSONAL

Nothing calls for introspection like half of your constituents telling you that they don't like the way you are reaching out to them.

If your alumni feel that you are going to corner them into donating money, they would much rather stay at home.

As the attention spans of your alumni become shorter every day, If you can stand out in the noise only if you make sure that your information is personal, relevant and interesting.

Show them all the effort that is going into your planning. Create a page on your alumni website, share it on social media.

Make it personal & go social!

49% of millenial alumni did not like the way they were asked for money
_ [2]

Ask them to give where they live:

Millennials are the first digital native citizens. Meaning they spend a significant portion of their waking lives on the internet. Their expectations and experiences are shaped by the world around them.

With providers like Amazon and Uber driving their online experiences everyday they have every right to expect their schools to be on par with the other walks of their lives.

We can definitely say that these advancements in technology encourage Millennials to expect effortless on-demand experiences when they purchase something. They expect the same from their giving experience. Your young alumni are online, and it is an effective ecosystem for them to connect with the world around them.

It comes down to this : If you want to be a part of their world, you need to go online.

PART TWO : MILLENIALS AND THEIR IMPACT

For starters, make your messaging personal. Show them all that is going into the planning. Create a page on your alumni website, share it on social media.

PART THREE
DIGITAL IS NOW DEFAULT
– GO ONLINE

PART THREE : DIGITAL IS NOW DEFAULT - GO ONLINE
SOCIAL MEDIA AUDIENCE ON THE RISE

Recent studies by the Case Foundation reveal that Millennials associate with a cause beginning with smaller actions rather than diving into a long-term commitment. This is the generation of people who are more motivated to "like" a Facebook page or share a video before participating in higher engagement. However, with constant fuel to their inspiration, they develop longstanding relationships and give wholeheartedly while encouraging their near and dear ones to contribute too! A large part of this inspiration comes from peers and social media.

Generation X has also caught on to the social media buzz of late. They witnessed the exponential rise of technology. Even the generation of baby boomers, who are often cited as the most generous givers, are not far behind. Social media is turning out to be the common thread between three generations by bringing them together on the same platform.

The entire world coming together online holds massive potential for alumni relations to leverage.

By 2018, the global population of social media users is projected to grow to 2.44 billion or 33% of the world population.

This is the generation of people who are more motivated to "like" a Facebook page or share a video before participating in higher engagement.

PART THREE : DIGITAL IS NOW DEFAULT - GO ONLINE

PERCENTAGE OF GLOBAL POPULATION ON SOCIAL NETWORKS

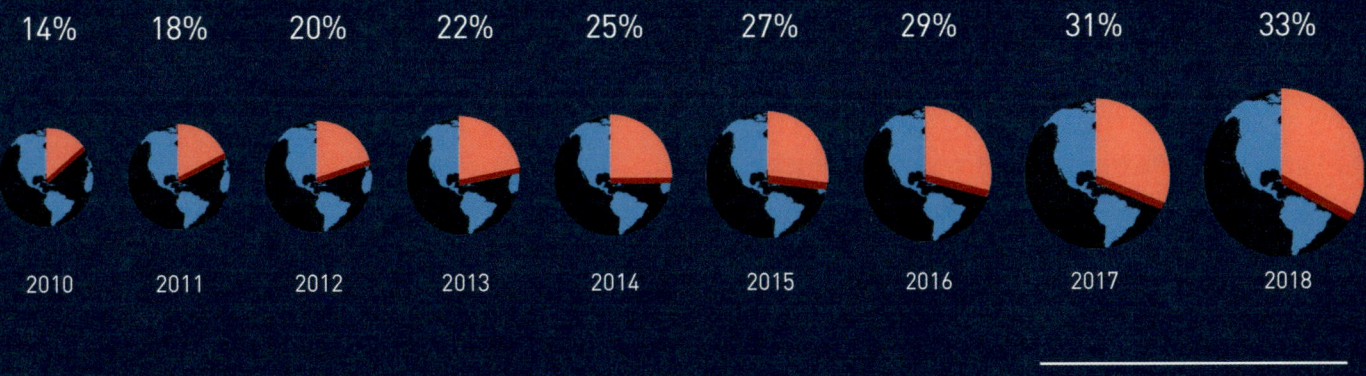

Projected

Source: Track Maven

PART THREE : DIGITAL IS NOW DEFAULT - GO ONLINE
GIVING ONLINE IS THE TREND

And if you think that this is a trend that represents only the current generation, we are wrong. The entire world is moving online and we should be ready to ride the wave.

An annual online study shows donors 75 and older now giving online. The silent generation gave more online gifts than other generations in the past 12 months.

PART THREE : DIGITAL IS NOW DEFAULT - GO ONLINE

ONLINE GIFTS PER YEAR BY SILENT VS ALL OTHER GENERATIONS

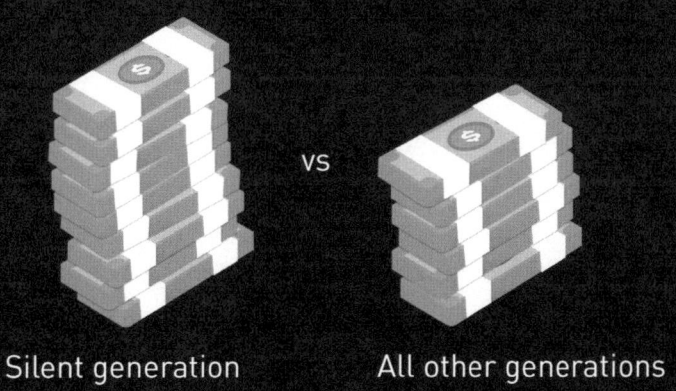

Silent generation vs All other generations

Source: Dunham+Company

PART THREE : DIGITAL IS NOW DEFAULT - GO ONLINE
SOCIAL PRESENCE IS THE WAY TO GO

Engagement itself has shifted definitions from bulky books describing stats to interactive videos conveying the same message but more effectively that retains the viewer's attention. Information spreads to people now at a skyrocketing pace via social media.

However, once they engage via social media, people prefer donating through a secure online portal. It is clear that social media tools aid in creating the first engagement option but they should be backed by engagement platforms and Giving channels to serve the greater goal.

The key takeaway here is that through social media, people play a huge role in drawing like-minded individuals towards giving to the cause of their choice.

And it's entirely in the hands of an organization to equip these generations of people with the right content to resonate with their cause and the right online platform to contribute to it.

This is a golden chance to make the most of your social presence and hit that home run for future engagement goals!

PART THREE : DIGITAL IS NOW DEFAULT - GO ONLINE

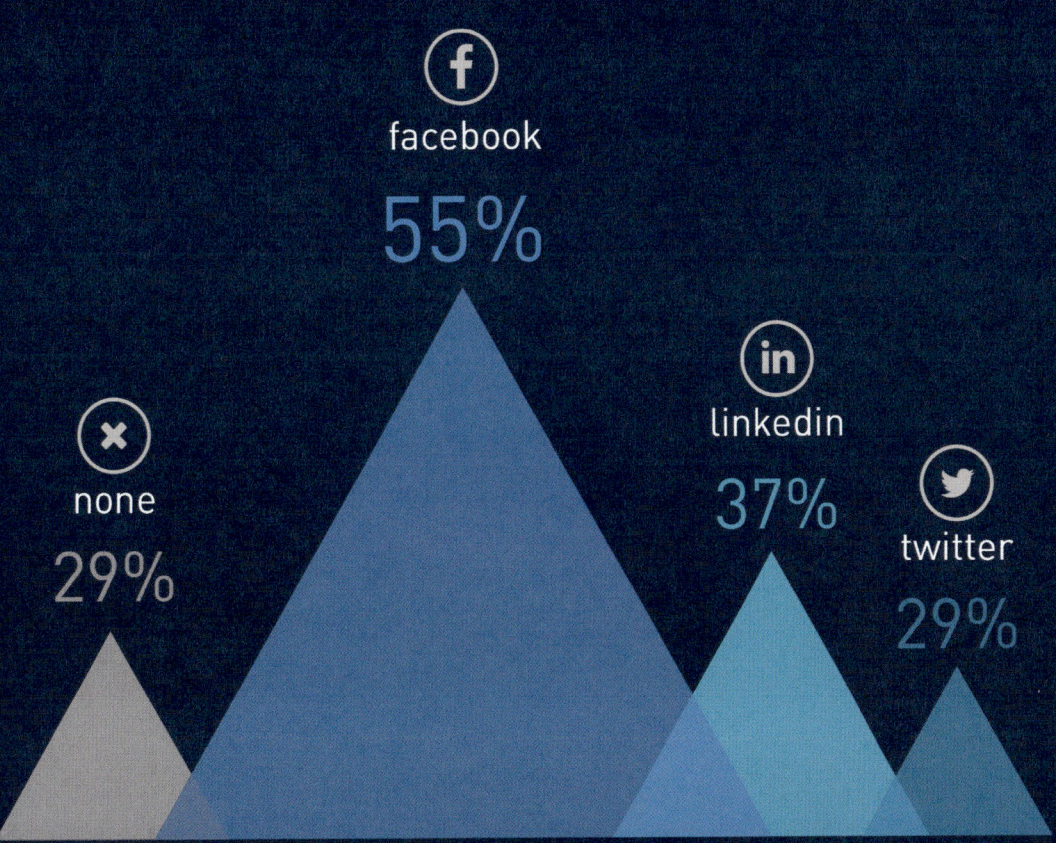

Source: Millennial Alumni Report - The Chronicle of Philanthropy (2014)

PART FOUR

DEDICATED ALUMNI MANAGEMENT PLATFORMS

PART FOUR : DEDICATED ALUMNI MANAGEMENT PLATFORMS
WHAT'S THE NEXT MOVE ?

The thriving ecosystem of alumni on social networks is commendable, indeed. For a school with a small close-knit group of alumni, connecting and interacting over Facebook or LinkedIn seems adequate. However, as your alumni base grows with each graduating class, keeping up with 45,000 people's lives is quite a daunting task for an alumni relations officer. Add to that multiple groups on innumerable social media websites, and one is bound to lose out on the vital information that matters. The need for a centralized alumni management platform is inevitable.

Migrating from sheets of alumni data to an all-accessible online database is a great start. You can step it up a notch through a dedicated platform for your school to interact with alumni that converts your database into a secure, active online community that you control. Alumni are an invaluable asset to a school, so nurturing a bond with them is essential. They could turn out to be job givers, excellent mentors and mainly, they carry your school's name, and with it, a legacy. A community exclusively for your school's alumni will reignite pride and a sense of belonging associated with your alma mater.

PART FOUR : DEDICATED ALUMNI MANAGEMENT PLATFORMS

A DEDICATED ALUMNI ENGAGEMENT (COMMUNITY) PLATFORM

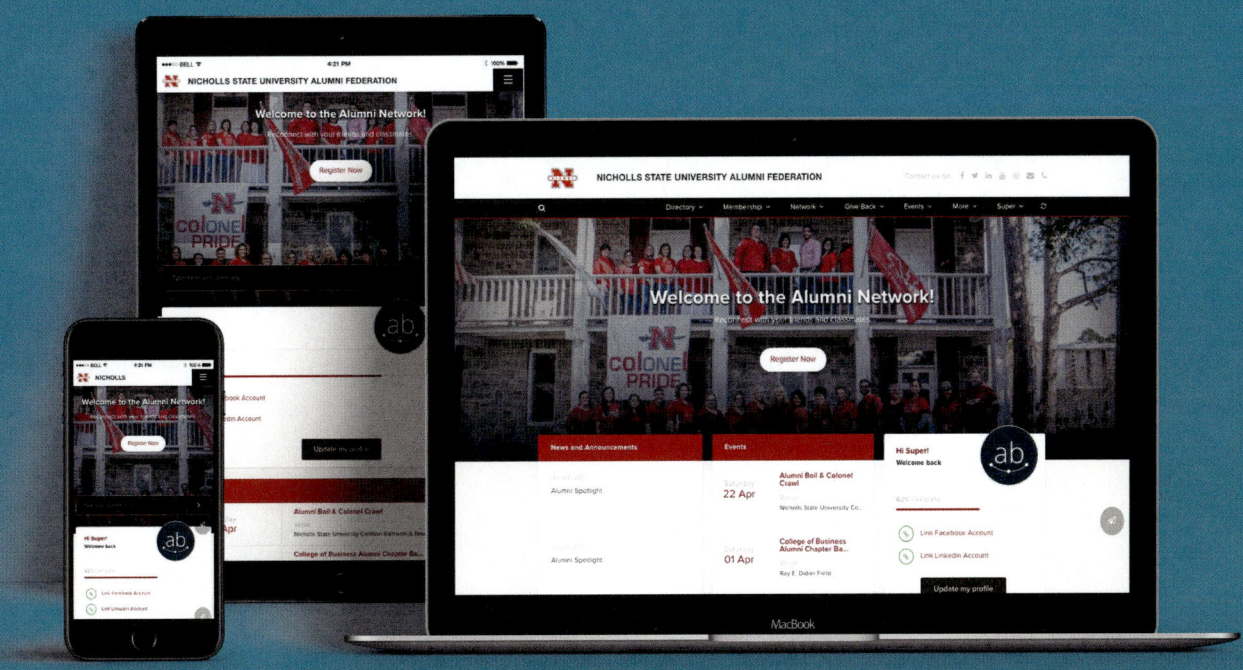

PART FOUR : DEDICATED ALUMNI MANAGEMENT PLATFORMS
WHAT DOES AN ALUMNI MANAGEMENT PLATFORM HOLD IN STORE FOR YOU?

Updated Database:
You no longer have to worry about getting bogged down with having to rummage through years of alumni data to put together a list. The online platform has it sorted for you with a simple search. This effectively leaves you with valuable time on your hands to build meaningful relationships with your alumni.

Effective Communication:
The integration of alumni's social media accounts with their profiles on the platform keeps you abreast about which of your alumni landed their dream jobs, married their high school sweethearts, made scientific breakthroughs or moved to a city near you. This enables you to effortlessly stay in touch with them and make them feel valued by your school.

Careers:
You can connect the job seekers directly with employers to provide continuous value to your alumni. This allows you to scale this effort up to serve a large number of your alumni.

Mentorship:
It also serves as the perfect platform for alumni to give back to their schools by mentoring students who in turn will do the same for future students, thus starting an active cycle of giving back.

Reunions:
Plan your next reunion around an exciting new theme based on the rich data from your alumni's interests collected by an array of filters on your alumni management software. It also takes the burden of putting together a mailing list off your hands by enabling you to send out invites to the whole any particular class, enabling you to invest your time in planning out the intricate details of the event.

PART FOUR : DEDICATED ALUMNI MANAGEMENT PLATFORMS

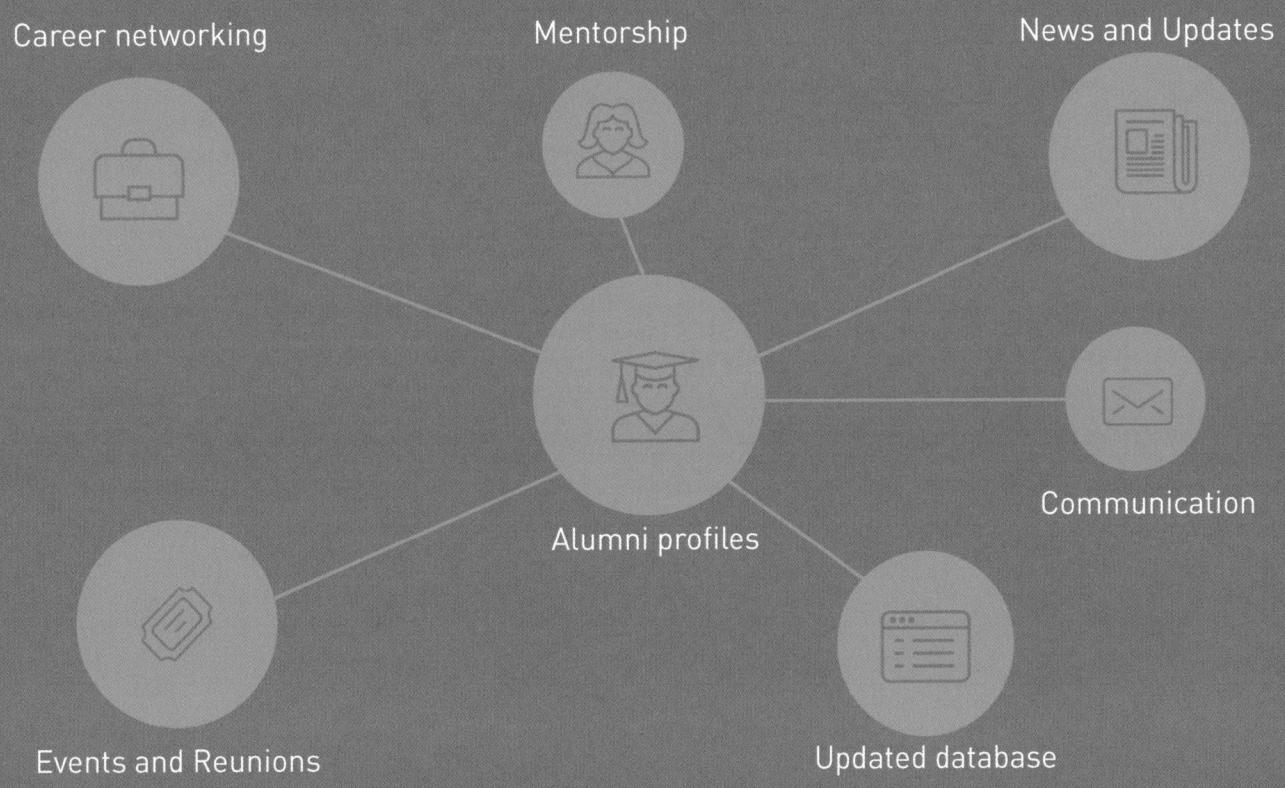

PART FOUR : DEDICATED ALUMNI MANAGEMENT PLATFORMS
MAKE MORE WITH LESS

1. Time:
Let's face it, you have a lot on your plate. We tend to take care of house keeping/administrative tasks first and then work on our relationships with alumni. A dedicated platform will make these administrative tasks easier - giving you time to focus on what really matters -building relationships with your Alumni.

2. Talent:
It doubles up as your personal alumni assistant by producing detailed analytics of which of your alumni attended most events, which class engages actively with your school; elaborate reports on students found jobs or by mentors, and gives you all the more reason to toast to the success of your latest fundraiser or reunion!

3. Treasure:
With more than 62% of Millennials preferring to donate online it helps if you are at the top of your game to make things easier for your alumni to give back.- [3]

It makes sense to discuss in detail on online giving as it is one of the most talked about subjects in the past year. Schools require their alumni's support now more than ever and the good news is that your alumni are willing to help you. It is only a matter of what we can do to make the most of it. We have a few interesting insights on this direction in the next chapter.

PART FOUR : DEDICATED ALUMNI MANAGEMENT PLATFORMS

Alumni are an invaluable asset to a school and nurturing a bond with them is essential. They could turn out to be job givers, excellent mentors and mainly, they carry your school's name and with it, a legacy.

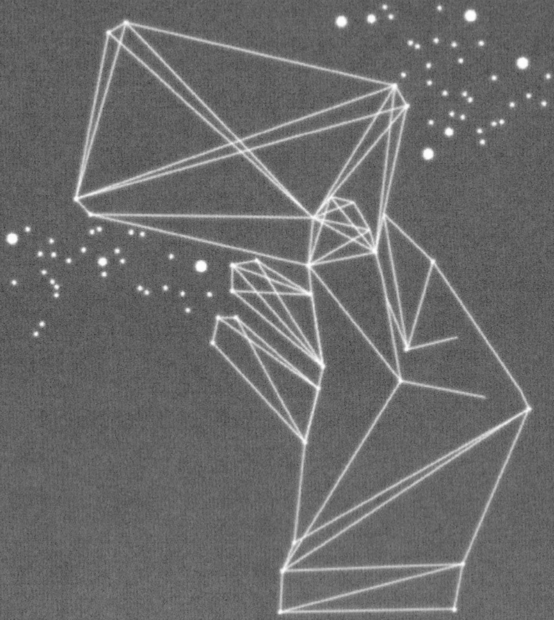

PART FIVE
ONLINE GIVING

PART FIVE : ONLINE GIVING
HOTTEST FORM OF GIVING

2016 has not been a great year for giving in the United States, growing only by 1 % which is even less than that previous year. But the silver lining is that there has been a considerable increase in online giving as a whole although the overall growth is slow.

Even though online giving accounts for only 7.3% of the total giving, there are two primary reasons why online giving is the best avenue to invest your time and resources.

1. It is the hottest form of giving right now!
Online giving in the Education sector has risen by an amazing 12.3 % to 15 % in last two years. - [4]

2. It has seen the largest adoption rate in the last few years.
62% of donors worldwide prefer to give online. - [5]

Simple math tells us that:
The average conversion rate on donation and giving pages is 10 % as per a report based on data from Blackbaud Online Express - [6]

- Assuming this conservative conversion rate of 10 % for every 1,000 visitors, you will have 100 donors.

The same report also shows that the conversion rate can become as high as 33% for mobile responsive pages.

- For the same 1,000 visits to your online donation form, if 30% of them convert to donors, you'll have 300 donors. That's a 200% improvement!

And depending on your average gift amount, this could equate to a significant increase for your organization.

The change in the world of alumni relations is very visible now with more schools moving towards online giving. We discovered a few roadblocks schools face during this transition from traditional giving to online giving.

PART FIVE : ONLINE GIVING

2015 and 2016 ONLINE GIVING TRENDS BY SECTOR (YOY GROWTH)

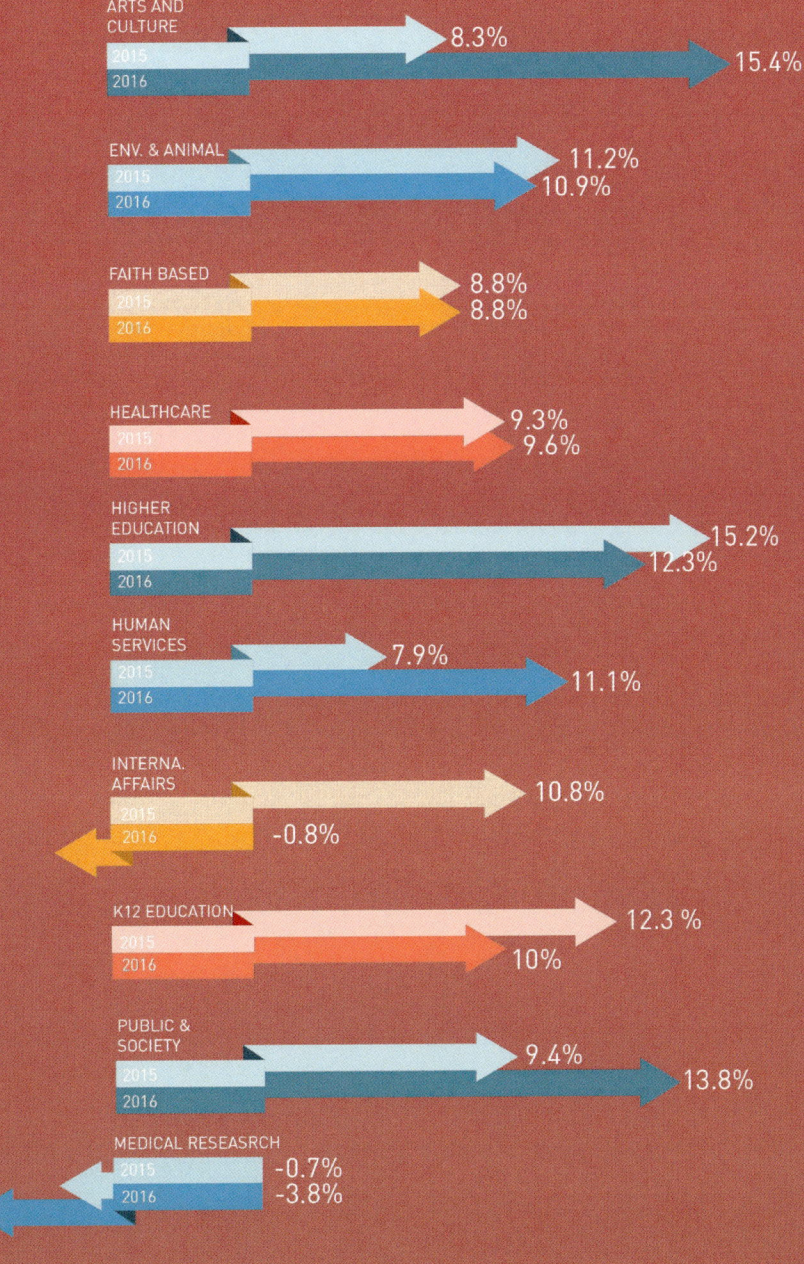

ARTS AND CULTURE
- 2015: 8.3%
- 2016: 15.4%

ENV. & ANIMAL
- 2015: 11.2%
- 2016: 10.9%

FAITH BASED
- 2015: 8.8%
- 2016: 8.8%

HEALTHCARE
- 2015: 9.3%
- 2016: 9.6%

HIGHER EDUCATION
- 2015: 15.2%
- 2016: 12.3%

HUMAN SERVICES
- 2015: 7.9%
- 2016: 11.1%

INTERNA. AFFAIRS
- 2015: 10.8%
- 2016: -0.8%

K12 EDUCATION
- 2015: 12.3%
- 2016: 10%

PUBLIC & SOCIETY
- 2015: 9.4%
- 2016: 13.8%

MEDICAL RESEASRCH
- 2015: -0.7%
- 2016: -3.8%

Source: Blackbaud-Annual Charitable Giving Report - 2015- 2016

PART FIVE : ONLINE GIVING
WHY DON'T YOUR ALUMNI GIVE ONLINE ?

There can be multiple reasons why you are not receiving as many gifts as you should. We designed a simple test for online giving pages where we measure your giving page's effectiveness with that of the Stanford University's giving page, arguably the best in the business, on a few factors including,

- **Mobile Friendliness**
- **Ease of use**
- **Security Assurances**
- **Focus on the cause**

Do you know how your school is performing against the industry standards and how much money your Giving page is potentially losing?

Friction points:
These are the various invisible red flags on your giving page that are stopping your alumni from donating there. We have discussed the most important of the lot in table on the right.

Where is the money lost?
For every 1,000 donors visiting your page only 6% i.e 60 of the are donating due to these friction points. And reports suggest that by reducing these friction points the percentage of donors can go as high as 33% i.e 330 gifts for every 1000 people visiting your page.

With the average online donation amount being as high as $128 there can be a potential gift loss of $35,000 for every 1,000 visitors.

All this differences in these numbers could easily be because of the donor friendly page that you don't gave because it is so easily overlooked. [4]

PART FIVE : ONLINE GIVING

Focus on what matters

At least 50% of your alumni may not spend more than 120 Seconds on the giving page. Does your giving page make it simple enough to find and click the donate button?

One thing at a time

Avoid multiple Call-To-Actions (CTAs) on the donation page. The only thing your Alum has to see there is the Give option. Nothing more, nothing less.

One click one gift

It should not be more than a click to donate on your giving page.

Mobile is the new smart

When 62% of your donors are smart phone users, it is important to ensure that both the emails and the Giving Pages linked to the emails are mobile friendly.

A Reason to give now

Give your Alum a reason to give now. Show them how the donations would indeed help a student who could not afford school without the scholarships or how their old basketball team needs their help.

Thank them

We saw that almost every single schools thanked their Alum after making a donation but to just thank a person for their gift is probably not enough. A short personalized e-mail would go a long way than a long general thank you note.

Test, measure and improvise

There is always room for improvement and the best way to do that is keep experimenting &improvising as you go.

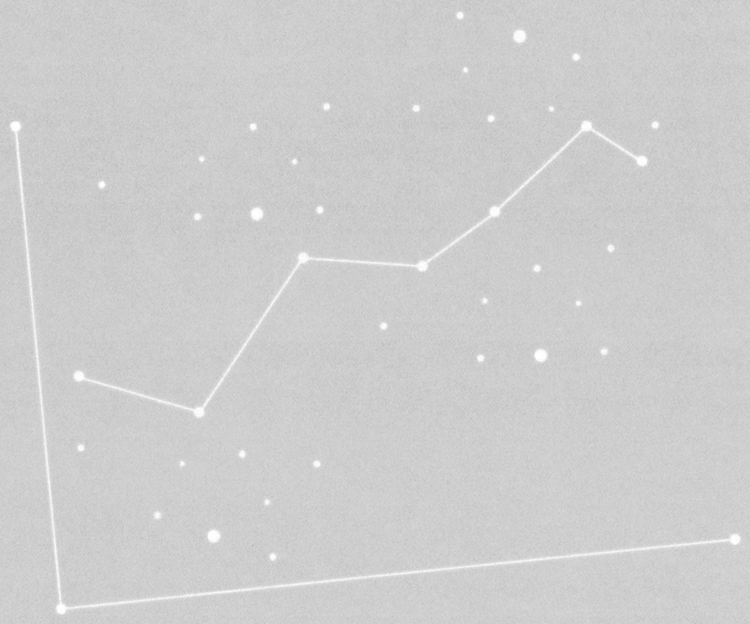

PART SIX

DATA DRIVEN DECISIONS WIN

PART SIX : DATA DRIVEN DECISIONS WIN
DATA SHOULD BE AT HEART

Gone are the days when alumni associations must spend most of their time and resources on social activities such as homecoming and reunions. They are now responsible for advancing our institutions through fundraising, recruitment, and research, enhancing student life and helping students and alumni find jobs. They are now strategists, and the goals they set must generate measurable results that greatly benefit the institution.

We believe that data should be at the heart of strategic decision-making in institutions, whether they are huge universities or high schools. Data can provide insights that help you answer your key questions (such as 'what do my alumni want?'). Data leads to insights; alumni relations and Development offices can turn those insights into decisions and actions that improve their quality of work. This is the power of data.

During our meetings with hundreds of alumni professionals across the country, two important questions that always emerged from our discussion were:

1. How engaged are our alumni, and

2. How can we increase the current level of alumni engagement and alumni giving?

We cannot tell you that there is a single answer or method that holds true in every institution, but thanks to our wonderful partner schools we learned some great insights from the world of alumni relations.

Data ⟶ Insights ⟶ Decisions

PART SIX : DATA DRIVEN DECISIONS WIN

Data leads to insights; Alumni Relations and Development offices can turn those insights into decisions and actions that improve their quality of work. This is the power of data.

PART SIX : DATA DRIVEN DECISIONS WIN
STAY UPDATED

The first step is to gauge the accuracy of your data. "You're only as good as the data you keep" has become a modern day mantra in many industries. It has certainly held true in the case of alumni relations for decades. But the challenge here is big.

Only 20.3% of the schools have updated data of their alumni.
_[1]

Your alumni change jobs all the time. They take on new positions at current companies. They switch to new companies. They move to a new city. Even worse, their email IDs, phone numbers and addresses also change often. How do you keep track of all this changing information?

Well, there are several approaches to solving this issue. We have tabulated a few and our observations about them.

As you can see from the table to your right, the key is to be able to do all of this seamlessly without having the alumni do everything manually each time something changes. Facebook and LinkedIn both provide interfaces to access these changes. The challenge is to build integrations with those interfaces and keep up with the changes on those interfaces as new technology and methods develop.

The best and easiest way is to outsource or buy software that takes care of all these nuances and provide you an easy-to-use system.

APPROACHES	SCALABILITY	RELIABILITY	FIND LOST ALUMNI	COST EFFECTIVE
A form on your web page	Medium	No	No	Yes
Calling your alumni	Low	Yes	No	No
Updating information at events	Low	Yes	No	Yes
Hire data enrichment services	Medium	No	No	No
Database managers tracking LinkedIn manually	Low	No	No	No
Facebook and LinkedIn auto update system	Yes	Yes	Yes	Yes

PART SIX : DATA DRIVEN DECISIONS WIN
MEASURING ENGAGEMENT AND IMPACT

Here we are, back to the original question. How do we measure alumni engagement? We agree that there is no easy way to do this. There are a lot of institutions that came up with their own ways of doing this. Data from surveys, personal interviews, postcards and many other sources have been used to predict the engagement levels.

One such institution that leads the way with outstanding work pertaining to this area is theThe University of Waterloo - Science behind alumni mangement. They have collected 24 items that indicated a person was more likely to be engaged and five items that meant that he or she was more likely to be disengaged. Engaged alumni are donors, have their job titles on file, have children attending the institution, and participate in events. Disengaged alumni are likely to have a bad address on file or "do not email" or "do not contact" solicit codes.

They decided that the two best predictors of impact on the institution were executive job titles and previous giving. These two data points were easy to apply to all records, and they could apply a sliding scale of impact to each. They added the predictive impact score (out of 100) for each alumnus and alumna in the database. They consider a score above 50 high and worthy of further research.

PART SIX : DATA DRIVEN DECISIONS WIN

WATERLOO COLLEGE ALUMNI BREAKDOWN

Impact ↑

Potential Leaders
3,346 Alumni	3%
% Donated	64%
Avg. no. of gifts	7
Avg. lifetime giving	$737
Total giving as group	$2,465,014
% of total giving pool	2%

low engagement • high impact

Leaders
1,248 Alumni	<1%
% Donated	96%
Avg. no. of gifts	48
Avg. lifetime giving	$94,897
Total giving as group	$118,437,030
% of total giving pool	78%

high engagement • high impact

Sleepers
128,823 Alumni	87%
% Donated	30%
Avg. no. of gifts	2
Avg. lifetime giving	$158
Total giving as group	$20,331,979
% of total giving pool	13%

low engagement • low impact

Champions
12,481 Alumni	9%
% Donated	48%
Avg. no. of gifts	12
Avg. lifetime giving	$819
Total giving as group	$10,219,003
% of total giving pool	7%

high engagement • low impact

Engagement →

PART SIX : DATA DRIVEN DECISIONS WIN
INCREASING ALUMNI ENGAGEMENT AND GIVING

A "one size fits all" plan may not work in the current scenario as different generations of alumni demand a different approach. With so many alumni and so little time to spend on each individual alum, engagement strategies based on age and generation hold the key to a life-long connection.

In a data-driven world, life-stage segmentation of constituents is the most trend we are observing now. Making use of this data, Alumni/Advancement offices can categorize their constituents into various segments and maximize the probability of giving.

Schools that customize their alumni engagement strategies based on age and generations prepare the right message based on those alumni's age, affinity, and generation, among other factors, to connect to them.

Of course, these are only baby steps towards a more robust and well-defined engagement strategy. After you have all the data and insights on your alumni, the next logical step is to customize your message to your alumni. Even with all your data and reports, unless you get your message across to your alumni your efforts will be in vain.

What you say is what they see!

PART SIX : DATA DRIVEN DECISIONS WIN

LIFE STAGE SEGMENTATION AND GROUPS

Young	Family	Mature
Singles and couples < 45 No children	Singles and couples 25-54	Singles and couples < 45 Childless
Y1 Midlife success	F1 Accumulated wealth	M1 Affluent empty nesters
Y2 Young achievers	F2 Young Accumulators	M2 Conservative class
Y3 Striving singles	F3 Mainstream Families	M3 Cautious couples
	F4 Sustaining Families	M4 Sustaining seniors

↑ Affluence

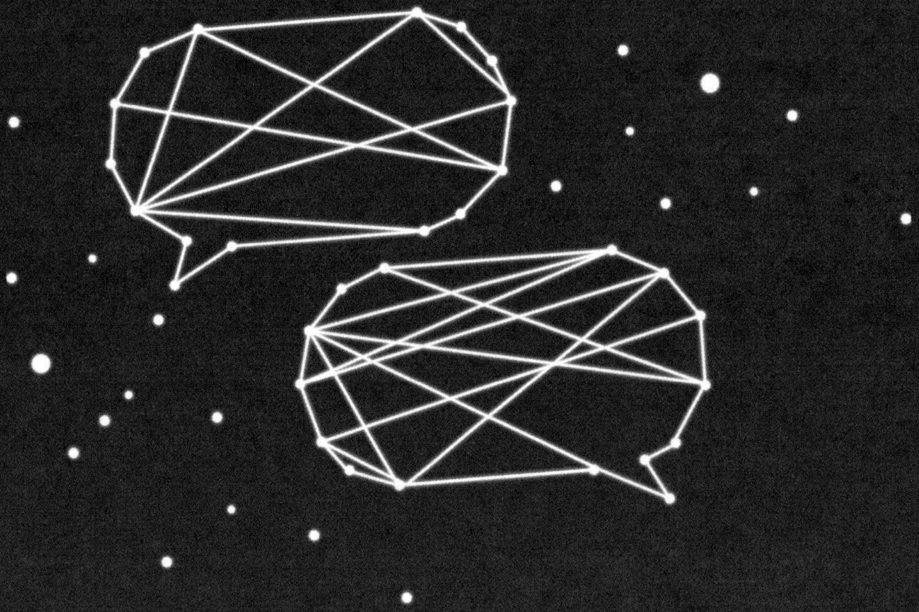

PART SEVEN

COMMUNICATION IS A TWO WAY STREET

PART SEVEN : COMMUNICATION IS A TWO WAY STREET
REACHING ALUMNI

Here is a secret about communication - it takes at-least two people to do it right. We agree that this is the oldest lesson in the book and continues to be the golden rule for any successful communication with your alumni. But let us try to view this notion in a new light.

Are you reaching out to your alumni because it meets their needs or because it's what you've always done?

In other words, is tradition preventing you from being strategically relevant in today's world?

Getting the right message to the right people at the right time is crucial in strengthening alumni relationships with the university, the association, and other alumni.

An increasing number of alumni communications offices are brainstorming and refocusing their activities on strategic priorities versus simply reacting to and serving all the organization's communications demands.

There are three parts of this puzzle,

1. **Right Message**
2. **Right Person**
3. **Right Medium**

Let us take a closer look on how these parts pan out.

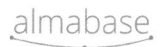

PART SEVEN : COMMUNICATION IS A TWO WAY STREET

Are you reaching out to your alumni because it meets their needs or because it's what you've always done?

PART SEVEN : COMMUNICATION IS A TWO WAY STREET
RIGHT MESSAGE

How many times has your team asked itself: 'What should we send to our alumni?' Our guess is very often. Now when was the last time your team asked itself: 'what do our alumni want to see?

Give your alumni a reason to come back.

Remember that your alumni are bombarded with tons of messages every day. You are not competing with your fellow schools because your competitors here are the 1.2 million non-profits vying for that short but precious attention span of your alumni. You need to stay clear of that noise to get noticed.

PART SEVEN : COMMUNICATION IS A TWO WAY STREET

You are not competing with your fellow schools because your competitors here are the 1.2 million non-profits vying for that short but precious attention span of your alumni

PART SEVEN : COMMUNICATION IS A TWO WAY STREET
RIGHT PERSON

Schools that have been around for at least 50 years or more have a melange of alumni spread across different generations and diverse backgrounds. Hence, it's important to have targeted communication with particular group of alumni.

During a student's enrollment at your school they develop and nurture life-long interests through clubs and groups.

These interests form memories and these memories are how alumni will remember your school for years to come.

For example, reaching out specifically to basketball enthusiasts in various graduating classes instead of all the alumni of only one class will elicit a better response for your school's annual basketball game.

Sharing a common platform of interest will enable alumni from different backgrounds to connect well.

PART SEVEN : COMMUNICATION IS A TWO WAY STREET

Sharing a common platform of interest will enable alumni from different backgrounds to connect well.

PART SEVEN : COMMUNICATION IS A TWO WAY STREET
RIGHT MEDIUM

In the 2016 Survey of Social Media in Advancement, nearly nine out of ten respondents did not hesitate to say that social media is a more important part of the communications and marketing efforts at their institutions. But, measuring the potential of such important communication and engagement channels is not an easy task without a deeper study on their implications.

Mail has worked great in the past, But very few millennials have a postal address they check and respond to regularly. For a generation that grew up with the internet, e-mails have worked great and have proven to be the most used and reliable form of communication today. Social networks like Facebook, LinkedIn,and Twitter are a great way to engage when you want to segment further by age, affinity, interests, etc.

Using the right channels helps you target the right alumni segment. Tracking e-mails and analyzing reply rates provide you with a lot of data to work with. Data leads to insights; alumni relations and Development offices can turn those insights into decisions and actions to make their alumni love their correspondence.

PART SEVEN : COMMUNICATION IS A TWO WAY STREET

TOP 5 SOCIAL MEDIA USED IN ALUMNI ADVANCEMENT - 2014,15,16

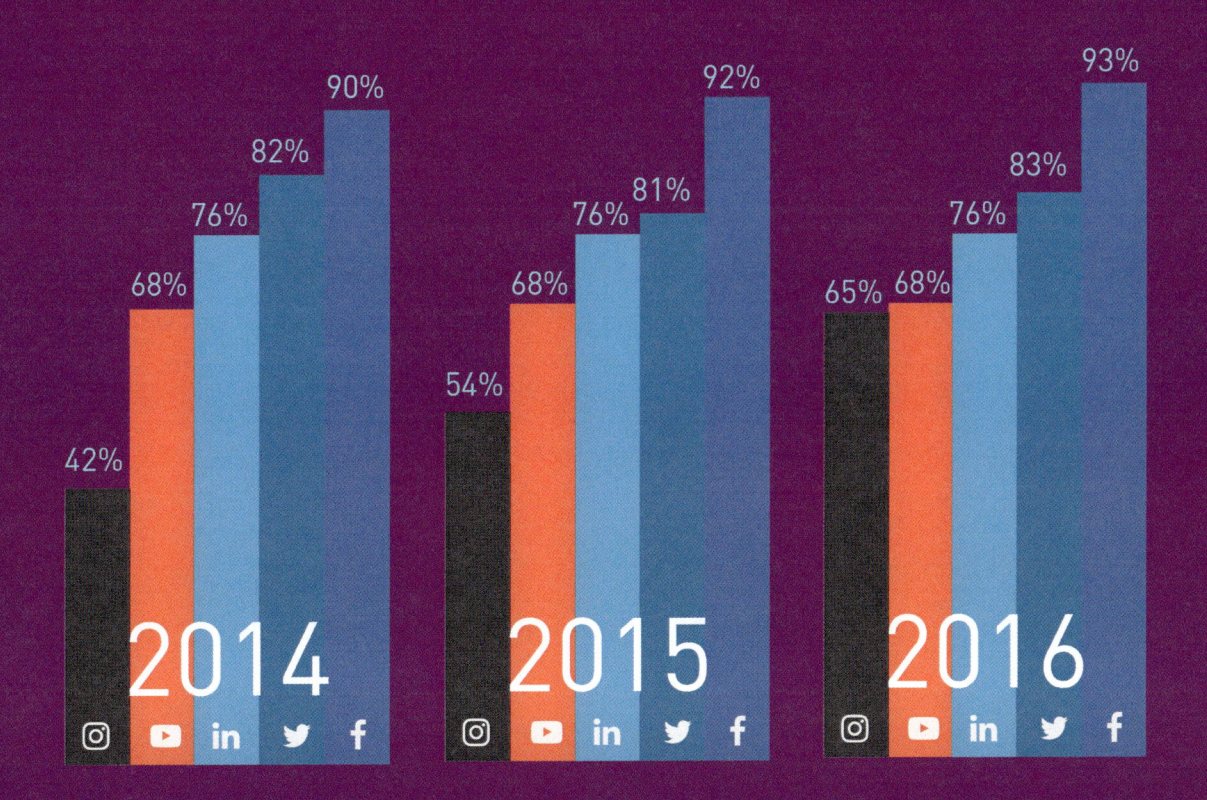

2014
- Instagram: 42%
- YouTube: 68%
- LinkedIn: 76%
- Twitter: 82%
- Facebook: 90%

2015
- Instagram: 54%
- YouTube: 68%
- LinkedIn: 76%
- Twitter: 81%
- Facebook: 92%

2016
- Instagram: 65%
- YouTube: 68%
- LinkedIn: 76%
- Twitter: 83%
- Facebook: 93%

Source: Paying to Play- Social Media in Advancement 2016 Report

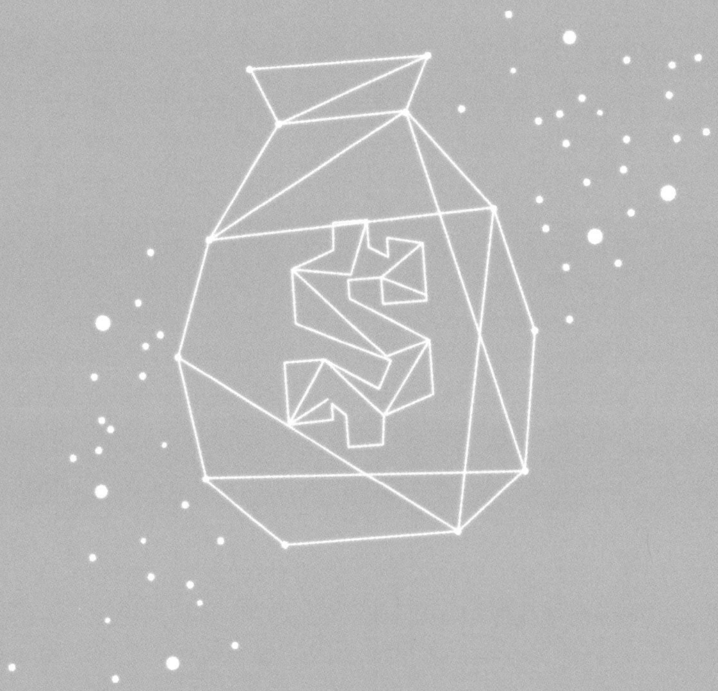

PART EIGHT
BUDGETING BLUES

PART EIGHT : BUDGETING BLUES
SAVE YOUR PROGRAMMING BUDGET

With increasing demands from development officers to find long-term solutions to their funding dilemmas, alumni relations executives likewise are having to respond by developing lifelong engagement tactics instead through more expensive, less effective, and short-term focused programs with diminishing returns. Life-long value drives life-long loyalty.

Most of your alumni spend a lot of time on the internet, and it's a growing number every single day. Your alumni relations team needs to pay attention to this because traditional alumni engagement strategies do not make the cut anymore. alumni have a bigger choice of the causes they can impact, and if you want them to pick your cause, you need to provide them enough value to get their attention.

Various schools have already started the process of involving technology to offset the budget constraints.

"A large community of educational institutions have already started investing in technology to support their online alumni communities: however, most are not satisfied with their current technology and 28% plan to invest in new online community technology in the next two years"
_ [8]

What is the ROI from an online community?
Before we get there, let us take a look at some interesting numbers on school budgeting.

The Staffing & Budget Benchmarks -2016 report by VAESE shows that

For schools with 1,000-25,000 alumni

The total budget of alumni relations (includes Salaries/benefits) is $123,337
The total programming budget is $91,858
The total percent of total budget dedicated to programming is 74%

For schools with 25,000-50,000 Alumni

The total budget of alumni relations (includes Salaries/benefits) is $266,744
The total programming budget is $156,367
The total percent of total budget dedicated to programming is 59%

PART EIGHT : BUDGETING BLUES

ACTIVITIES COVERED BY ALUMNI RELATIONS BUDGET 2012 VS 2015

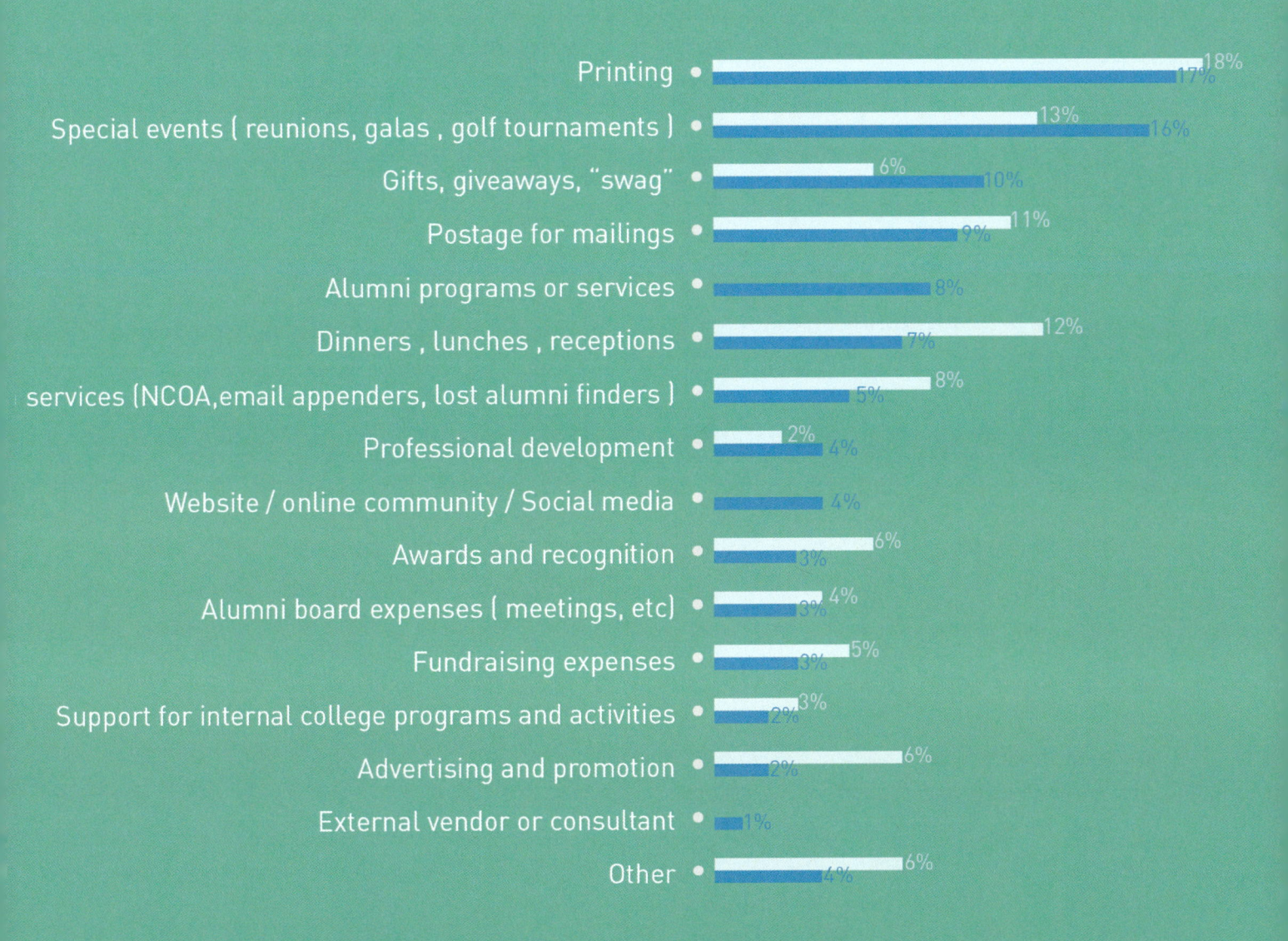

Activity	2012	2015
Printing	18%	17%
Special events (reunions, galas, golf tournaments)	13%	16%
Gifts, giveaways, "swag"	6%	10%
Postage for mailings	11%	9%
Alumni programs or services		8%
Dinners, lunches, receptions	12%	7%
services (NCOA, email appenders, lost alumni finders)	8%	5%
Professional development	2%	4%
Website / online community / Social media		4%
Awards and recognition	6%	3%
Alumni board expenses (meetings, etc)	4%	3%
Fundraising expenses	5%	3%
Support for internal college programs and activities	3%	2%
Advertising and promotion	6%	2%
External vendor or consultant		1%
Other	6%	4%

Source: The Staffing & Budget Benchmarks -2016 report by VAESE

PART EIGHT : BUDGETING BLUES
SAVE YOUR PROGRAMMING BUDGET

Many school's alumni programming budgets are decreasing. Now, more than ever, advancement offices and alumni relations officers are subject to increasing economic and technological pressure. These pressures place tremendous burdens on senior advancement and alumni executives to make sound decisions about their budgets and staffing.

Before we dwell on the topic of ROI from online communities, have we ever thought about how much time and effort we spend in determining our return on investment from any of the following:

- Newsletters, magazines and other mailings sent to alumni

- Events like homecoming, reunions and award banquets

From our conversations with hundreds of alumni professionals across the country, very few of them perform a break-even analysis. Even less are determining if alumni are reading the newsletters or magazines sent. With magazines and newsletters you can't tell how many alumni are reading them or which stories were the most popular to gather feedback from your alumni. Events that are not hosted online involve a lot of manual work which in turn increases the overhead costs. An objective look at this spending, along with the other activities you host will help in developing a fresh, different perspective. Having said that, we don't want you to stop doing any of them; instead we are creating a new line of thought here.lot of manual work which in turn increases the overhead costs. An objective look at these along with the other activities you involve in will help in developing a fresh, different perspective. Having said that, we don't want you to stop doing any of them; instead we are creating a new line of thought here.

Here are 3 different areas where having a strategy for Online Engagement helps you save on your programming budget.
1. Increase in Giving & Donations
2. Reduction in Costs
3. Low Investment

Let us the see the ROI on Online Engagement:
ROI = (Return attributable to the investment – Investment) / Investment

Return = Increased Giving + reduction in costs

Investment = Time, resources, People

PART EIGHT : BUDGETING BLUES

Advancement offices and alumni relations officers are subject to increasing economic and technological pressure

PART EIGHT : BUDGETING BLUES
INCREASE IN YOUR GIVING & DONATIONS

Online Giving:
We can never have enough giving. There are always more scholarships to cater to, better equipment to be bought and the better experiences to be provided.

Membership fees:
This is one of the most traditional ways of giving back one's alma mater. But in the age of Uber and Amazon your alumni have every right and reason to expect a similar experience from you in collecting these fees. Meet them where they live, make the giving experience very easy and thank them properly for every donation they make.

Matching Gifts:
Matching gifts increase the capacity of your donors' contributions. Companies big, small, and everything in between, match gifts. Most programs are not only generous about giving money but are willing to donate to a broad spectrum of organization types.

PART EIGHT : BUDGETING BLUES

Meet them where they live, make the giving experience very easy and thank them properly for every donation they make.

PART EIGHT : BUDGETING BLUES
REDUCTION IN COSTS

1. Email vs snail mail
Snail mail is still important for the occasional message, but to be consistently reaching out to your alumni with valuable information, you need to adopt email. Even if you have 5,000 alumni and send one email per month instead of a snail mail piece, you are saving upwards of $5,000 each month.

2. Data updates
Your alumni outreach is only as effective as the accuracy of your data. If you don't have updated contact information for all your alumni, you are wasting a lot of money on dead addresses with no return. Online communities help you keep your database up-to-date and render your outreach more cost effective.

3. Alumni self-servicing
By enabling your alumni to connect and network with each other, you facilitate connections that provide value to your alumni without spending an extra dollar. Career advice and professional networking, location-based notifications for personal networking, mentorships for students — are all opportunities that you can enable for your alumni using an online community.
Again, remember, life-long value for your alumni drives life-long loyalty.

almabase

PART EIGHT : BUDGETING BLUES

Snail mail is still important for the occasional message, but to be consistently reaching out to your alumni with valuable information, you need to adopt email.

PART EIGHT : BUDGETING BLUES
INVESTMENT

Investment includes the people, time and financial costs tied to this online community.

Money
What is the cost involved in acquiring this online community? This includes all the set up fee and other overhead costs.

Staff
How much are you paying for your staff? This covers the salaries/pay of the staff involved in running the online community.

Time
What is the time invested in this? We are certain it would be way less than doing all these tasks manually.

Put them together and measure your ROI

ROI = (Return attributable to the investment – Investment) / Investment

We encourage you to use the formulas in this book to calculate your own office's ROI. From our experience with more than 100 schools across the globe, a lot of them saw that this is a very profitable equation for the schools who want to develop a life-long relationship with their alumni.

Advancement and alumni executives are faced with having to re-think how they will adapt to these new realities. Clearly, they will involve leveraging new technologies, but they will also have to adapt to an increasingly tech savvy, demanding, and service-oriented alumni constituency who are (and will be) far more ethnically and culturally diverse than ever before. And all these monumental changes must occur within the constraints of increasingly limited budgets would be the biggest challenge ahead of us.

PART EIGHT : BUDGETING BLUES

Advancement and alumni executives are faced with having to re-think how they will adapt to these new realities.

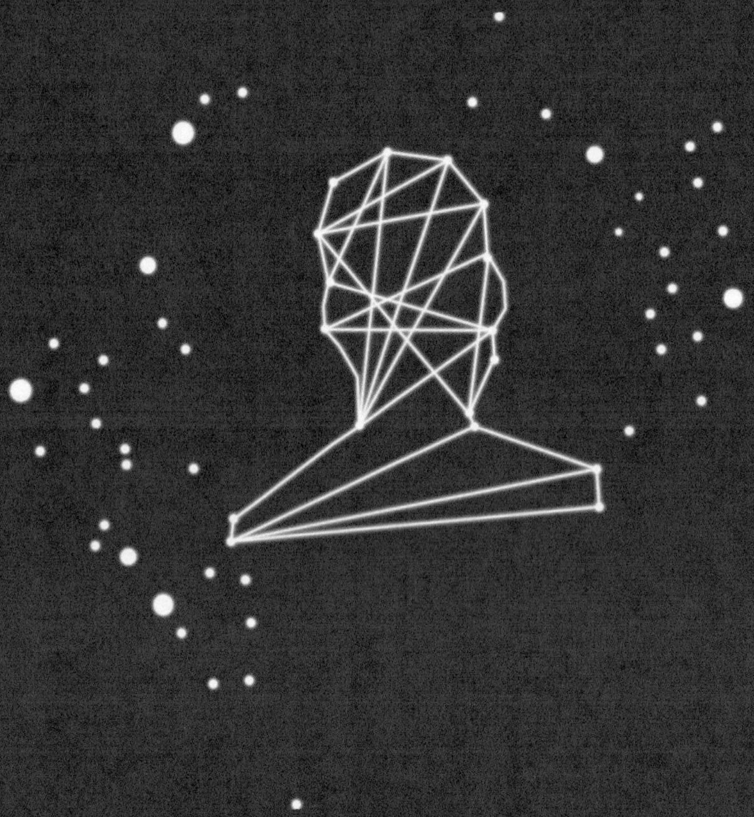

PART NINE

INSIGHTS INTO THE WORLD OF ALUMNI RELATIONS

INSIGHTS INTO THE WORLD OF ALUMNI RELATIONS

ALUMNI ASSOCIATION OF SCHOOL OF MEDICINE OF LOMA LINDA UNIVERSITY

Calvin Chuang
Executive Director,
Alumni Association,
School of Medicine of Loma Linda University

Calvin Chuang is one of our early supporters who has been with us for a long time. It was a steep learning curve for us working with LLUSMAA who guided us with their constructive feedback helping hundred other partner schools.

Jishin: Hey Calvin, thank you for meeting with us today. Could we start off by taking a look back into your journey to alumni relations?

Calvin: Yeah. My name is Calvin Chuang. I have been working as the Executive Director of the Loma Linda University School of Medicine Alumni Association for a year. Prior to that, I was working at the office as a documentary filmmaker. I got the opportunity to visit several countries. I did a documentary in Sierra Leone and Liberia on Ebola. I got to go to Africa a couple of times. And before that, I owned my own production company back in Australia.

Jishin: Things are probably quite different from what you were used to with media production. What does your typical work day look like now?

Calvin: My typical day looks like a lot of meetings - more than I've ever had to do before. As we are our own 501(c)(3) non-profit, everything runs through boards and committees. So I'm sitting on a lot of committees, and I sit and discuss what they want to do and they give me my marching orders and I carry them out. So, that involves a lot of e-mails, a lot of organizing and a lot of event planning. And I try to bring in some of my old skills like graphic design, promotion and marketing as well into the role.

On the big changes in the industry

Jishin: Is the paradigm shifting with alumni relations? What are some of the big changes that you have seen happening in the industry over the last few years?

Calvin: Good question. I think I'll expand that even more to nonprofits in general. What we're seeing is that people don't support nonprofits as much as they used to. There is a sharp decline. If you look at the research there's a sharp decline of support for nonprofits across the board. For alumni association that's even lesser support. Especially since you don't see a lot of (well we're not seeing a lot of) younger alumni support the organization.
What we are seeing is that younger alumni love to support causes. They'll support the things like the ice bucket challenge - those kinds of things. But the actual organization behind it, they won't know - They want a cause to support.
So what we've noticed is that we've had to change our strategy.
For the younger millennials who are passionate about causes - we can find causes for them to kind of sink their teeth into. While the older alumni still prefer supporting the association as it is.

Technology in Alumni Relations

Jishin: How or where do you think all of this – technology, online communities, giving - fits in with the broader perspective?

Calvin: It's actually been really interesting. This organization is approaching 100 years old. So it's gone through a lot of technological changes. In fact, not too long ago (probably about 15 years ago) I heard a previous employee say they were still using the typewriter in here. So it's gone through a big change. They've gone from typewriters to computers and now they're embracing the Internet and online activity.
What it has helped us do, though, is to cut down the amount that we spend to mail out. Earlier, we used a lot of mail outs, and now we're using a lot of emails - which has helped. We're able to track the e-mails and see who has opened them. Their community - the platform itself - has allowed us to see who's active and to monitor their progress and for moving forward. I think the big thing for us is that medical school which is the alumni association I belong to is a unique course in which these guys go through four years of intense training together. So there's

INSIGHTS INTO THE WORLD OF ALUMNI RELATIONS

a certain bond there. Having a platform where they can all get reconnected with each other and keep those bonds alive - that's really helpful for us moving forward.

Online Fundraising

Jishin: You guys have been doing some tremendous work with online fundraising. Where do you see online fundraising is headed?

Calvin: Online fundraising has been interesting as well. We've seen more recently that crowd-sourcing is becoming more popular with communities. That really just helps people to say "OK we're going to get this". And when they hit that goal - they're excited and then they want to get past that goal. We have some pretty ambitious donations or causes right now that we're trying to fill. And last week, we passed our student goal by 20 percent. So it's been really helpful just to see that money is coming in.

Jishin: How do you manage to steer technology and human aspect of Alumni Relations at LLUSMAA?

Calvin: In the past and I think even today - technology is a tool. It's a tool that we use to try and build the community at the end of the day. As an alumni association, we are simply a community. That is our product. If we don't have the community we don't have a product; we don't exist.

So what we're doing with technology is basically "Trying to get people to interact with the technology to build that community".

So, being able to contact classmates that they haven't seen is big.

Then, we have a program for students to reach out to alumni. They do an interview at trial - so they reach out to fellow alumni in those cities to provide free accommodation.

Those kinds of touch points and those kind of connections are what built our body as a community of medical alumni. So while technology is important, it helps facilitate that it's those connections that will actually help grow our relationship.

Data driven world!

Jishin: In this data driven world where do you see technology being a game changer for alumni relations in the short term?

Calvin: Good Question. I would say, from the perspective of this office, I can see technology benefiting us in making appropriate connections.

Making appropriate connections not only for financial giving, to ask for the right amount of dollars if we do a fundraising campaign.
But, to make appropriate connections when it comes to mentoring. To make appropriate connections when it comes to asking someone to essentially be on board for a specific cause. Having that data, and being able to look at that data, and that history - will allow us to make more appropriate decisions.
Right now we're basing it off what we know, what someone else said, or what little information we have. Which isn't bad, but now we can actually look at the data and say this person on paper is good, let's get a few references and let's connect up.
That way, I think making appropriate connections will help us build a community that is stronger and more vibrant.

Jishin: Am glad to hear that Calvin. With our shared love for technology and enthusiasm for Alumni Relations, we've always been excited about our relationship with you and the association.

Calvin: Yeah I know. It's been fun working with you guys. Really! Thank you for you and your team and what you guys have been doing for us!

Jishin: Thank you so much, Calvin! It's been great working with you as well.

Note: this is the abridged-version of the actual interview. You can find the full-length version of this interview on our site, https://blog.almabase.com/category/resources/

INSIGHTS INTO THE WORLD OF ALUMNI RELATIONS
NICHOLLS STATE UNIVERSITY

Jessica F. Harvey, M.A.
Assistant Director, Alumni Affairs
Nicholls State University

Katherine Gianelloni
Alumni Engagement Coordinator
Nicholls State University

Jishin: I've got Jessica and Katherine here with me who are two people who have been pivotal to changing the alumni relations ecosystem at Nicholls State University. They've been an amazing example of people who've adopted technology as a tool to nurture the human relationships in the community - I really find that inspiring. I'm really looking forward to talking to you guys.

To start off, I know that both of you guys are alumni of Nicholls right? How did how did you transition from being a student/alumni into your current roles here?

Katherine: So I was a student not long ago. I graduated and then traveled for a year. Then when I came back and I was searching for a job, this position was created. And then I came in. I feel like we're still adjusting that role even two years to the day. Every day it's changing! I think it is great when you get to meet all the alumni and each of them have their story just like I have mine and Jessica has hers. So it's been a really good transition.

Jessica: I got my degree here and in English and then I went on to get a master's degree in English as well. I worked in the retail sector for a year, and then the assistant alumni director position was opened up - which, at that time (nine years ago) was also a brand new position to alumni.
So we have created it and built it as we have gone along.
The same way, transitioning from a student to a grad student and then to being an alum in an alumni position has been interesting. I've always been interested in the communications I think in being an English major, I use a lot of those skills here!

Jishin: That's interesting. Jessica, can you tell me a little more about how things are right now as compared to how it was back then?

Jessica: Well, when I was here, my first semester, we were still turning in handwritten papers for a class and then we went to floppy disks. It is strange just saying that!
MySpace was kind of just getting started. For online communications, we were just using email.
I see that technology has completely grown from where – "We go hang out in person and call people on land lines" to how "Everything is on your cell phone and you hang out on Facebook". It's been amazing to watch it change. Also, it's fascinating to be part of that technology changing the work space and being able to apply it.

Jishin: What about you Katherine? I guess things are not that different from back when you were here, but any big changes just in the last few years?

Katherine: No, it really hasn't been any different. But it's been different to see the alums trying to adapt to the technology and trying to engage alums from different generations. Some of them prefer hand-written letters, some prefer mailings, some e-mail. And some just want to stop by for a cup of coffee. So that's been really interesting to adapt too.

On Technology in Alumni Relations

Jishin: That's interesting! Where do you see technology playing a role in all this?

83

INSIGHTS INTO THE WORLD OF ALUMNI RELATIONS

Katherine: So, especially in the next few months, I'd really like to expand the mentorship platform, and reach out to more alums to be able to sign up to be mentors.

Last year we started our very first "Colonel Connections" event (which was kind of like a speed networking event) between students and alums. We learned a lot. And I think it was very successful for the first time.

Jessica: I think with that growth, with students knowing what 'alumni' is from the start when they graduate they'll already be interested in coming back. They'll be more interested in being mentors themselves, and so they'll be more interested in staying connected with the university, and that's our whole goal! – To keep them connected.

Data driven world!

Jishin: Definitely. That makes sense! In all this, where do you see 'data' coming in and playing a bigger role in coming years?

Jessica: With data, we are definitely looking for figuring out where our alums are working. That's one of the big things that the university is starting to ask about. That's one of the big things that would make it easier for us to do specifically targeted pieces to those alums and their interests if we know where they are and what they're doing. So a big part of that is going to be figuring out more easily where they are. And I think that will help us enhance the personal connection too. When we know who they are, we can have those conversations with them.

Katherine: Yeah I definitely agree. Jessica handles a lot of the data for us and I think we tag team very well. She handles more of the data and me more of the engagement. So those two go hand in hand because without the data we can't engage them.

Dues based vs Campaign based Memberships

Jishin: Katherine, you are one of the recipients of the CASE District IV scholarships for this year! I'm sure that you have a lot of interesting insights from these conferences about alumni leadership.

Katherine: I think one of the interesting things that we're learning is about Dues based organizations versus a campaign based membership. We are currently dues based, with membership at different levels. A lot of other universities do something like a capital campaign and that's how they raise all their funds. So that's been very interesting. It's an idea that we have tossed around with our Alumni Federation Board.

Jishin: So if you were to pick one aspect where Online Engagement platforms have simplified your work, what would that be?

Katherine: The event module on Almabase is my favorite! It makes my job so much easier! Going from online forms, I can put it in Excel and track all of it. It?s been wonderful! Especially for our last event. We incorporated a bar crawl and a crawfish boil into one event. So we're tracking who signing up for what, what they're paying online. From that to actually seeing the alumni at the end made the whole event so much easier on me. So definitely, the event module's my favorite.

Jessica: From a tracking standpoint on my end - with the data and the financials. It has made it a lot easier.
I also love the way that we can integrate our social media. On Almabase, that's been perfect! We haven't gotten very far with the mentor platform. We're looking to keep moving forward with that. And I think that will really take off in the fall - when the students are back and we're all geared up for the summer. So I'm super excited about that too!

Jishin: Thank you so much. That's really amazing to hear! There?s so much excitement that it?s rubbing off on me as well! Thank you for your time both of you!

Note: this is the abridged-version of the actual interview. You can find the full-length version of this interview on our site, https://blog.almabase.com/category/resources/

INSIGHTS INTO THE WORLD OF ALUMNI RELATIONS
COLLEGE OF IDAHO

Sally Skinner
Director of Alumni and Parent Relations
College of Idaho

Lauren Aguas Bevill
Alumni and Parent Relations Coordinator
College of Idaho

Jishin: I've got Sally and Lauren from the College of Idaho here with me today. Can you please say a few words on how you got into this positions?

Lauren: Well I'm Lauren Bevill and I've been in alumni relations now for one year officially. I'm here at the College of Idaho. Before that, I was doing marketing in and merchandising for a major retailer and I kind of wanted to come back and be with people again. Since then we've been focusing on communication, events and then really having that home feeling for alumni.

Sally: I've been here at the college for five years. I re-potted myself (as one of our alumni said) in this career after working in elementary education for most of the rest of my life. So it's good to be back on campus for these five years. I've had to deal with alumni all along, but now to be in this spot really to grow the impact of alumni like has been a fun challenge.

On changing trends

Jishin: How has it(Alumni Relations) changed compared to when you were students or alumni?

Sally: Well for me it's changed significantly as it has been a long time. Social media has changed so many things that we do. Our alumni say to us, "You know, I don't really need to have to go to an event to get to see my friends. I know what they're doing pretty much every day, all the time" which is very different than when I graduated. We did have to get together to stay in touch.
So, that has dramatically changed from when I was a student and then a young alum.

Lauren: Oh absolutely. And you know even when I was a student, smartphones were just - they were new. I didn't have an iPhone until after I graduated from the college and now everything is so mobile and so connected. In the last 5 years, it's a totally different type of communication that we're having with our alumni. But we're trying to find that balance of not over communicating with them - via Facebook and email, and we've got a phonathon going on right now as well! So it's definitely different.

Online Communities

Jishin: So how do you see the role of online communities, online giving, phonathons etc? How do you put all those pieces together?

Lauren: I think it provides an easier way for alumni to connect with the college. The online community is where they can go to find out everyone, rather than looking on Facebook where they will have to search individually. I think for Online Giving as well- letting them go in there and make the choice of where they want to give the gift to, rather than calling and not knowing what they can do is important. We can now give them more information about where their money is going, or what it does - in one place. It's really all helpful.

Sally: I agree. For us, I think for some of the older alumni, a lot of them are on Facebook, but it gives them the another avenue to find people that they really haven't thought about for a long time. Probably the numbers, the percentage of people on social media is certainly less, for people in my generation.

INSIGHTS INTO THE WORLD OF ALUMNI RELATIONS

Key to successful Alumni Communities

Jishin: A specific question to you Sally, because you've been in the higher-ed space for quite a few years. What do you think is the key to a successful Alumni Community now?

Sally: It's a great question. You know for us our personal relationships are the key.
So what we certainly see is that technology is going to continue to drive us into places that we don't probably even know.
At the heart of our college and alumni relations is the personal relationship. That is what our graduates tell us over and over again. It was the community they built when they were here and the relationship they built with the faculty.

Lauren: I think it's more than just a matter of asking for money. For us, being in alumni relations. Our department specifically, we don't ask for money at any event that we do or any time that we're meeting with the alumni. It's all about cultivating that spirit. So that someday they'll reach into their pocket and give to us rather than us asking for money from them.
We really want to cultivate that Coyote pride so they love the college more and they want to come back.

Jishin: One of the interesting things that we believe, is that alumni are shifting from an obligation based relationship to a value based one with their college. Any thoughts on this?

Lauren: Actually, Sally has been working with our alumni and our group of parents to put together a service project - so that alumni can come back and give their time. These alumni that she's been meeting with, want to put together a group that comes to campus. Not only do the majority of them give back monetarily, but they want to come back and do more. They want to do anything - landscaping projects, they want to have a park in the campus and be more involved. Rather than just money, they want a purpose, they want to give value!

Sally: I think our alumni are out there doing great things. One of the things they love to do is mentor younger students. But right now, it really has depended on us to be that broker for that relationship. And that's one of the things that we do hope that online community can really help us with. To take out that middle man. So that we know - who's going to help, who needs help and be able to make that connection in a much more efficient way.

Jishin: Glad to hear that. That is something we believe in too. Thanks for all the interesting insights. It was great speaking with both of you.

Note: this is the abridged-version of the actual interview. You can find the full-length version of this interview on our site, https://blog.almabase.com/category/resources/

#STAY RELEVANT
CONCLUSION

We know that Alumni Relations is a tough job—after all, we're working with more than a hundred schools ourselves. We also know that there's no perfect, one-size-fits-all approach to alumni relations. Nevertheless, we firmly believe that we have the capability to take your existing channels and tactics and help you maximize their potential.

Keep your alumni's challenges, goals, and concerns at the top of your thoughts; provide value that solves their problems; nurture those relationships and engage them. Over time your Alumni would love you, again!

We hope that this small book will help you enrich your already thriving alumni community.

#STAY RELEVANT

#STAY RELEVANT
ABOUT THE GUIDE

Written by
Amar M
Director of Development, Almabase

Designed by
Manoj M
Product Designer, Almabase

Interviews by
Jishin C
Customer Success, Almabase

Made with ♥ in SF, NYC & BLR over ☕

#STAY RELEVANT
SPECIAL THANKS

Calvin Chuang,
Executive Director
Alumni Association,
School of Medicine of Loma Linda University

Jessica F. Harvey, M.A.
Assistant Director, Alumni Affairs
Nicholls State University

Katherine Gianelloni
Alumni Engagement Coordinator
Nicholls State University

Sally Skinner
Director of Alumni and Parent Relations
College of Idaho

Lauren Aguas Bevill
Alumni and Parent Relations Coordinator
College of Idaho

We would also like to thank the following firms for their research articles that helped us a lot in making this guide.

Sources:

[1] : VAESE Alumni Relations Benchmarking Study (2016)

[2] : Millennial alumni Report - The Chronicle of Philanthropy (2014)

[3] : 2016 Global NGO Online Technology Report

[4] : Blackbaud-Annual Charitable Giving Report - 2015

[5] : Blackbaud Annual Giving Report 2015, 2016

[6] : https://www.sparkrock.com/blog/2016-global-ngo-online-technology-report

[7] : NP Engage report on data from BlackBaud Online Express

[8] : Use of Technology for Development and Alumni Relations - CASE

[9] : Paying to Play- Social Media in Advancement 2016 Report

[10] : The University of Waterloo - Science behind Alumni Management

[11] : Eduventures' Alumni Pulse

Partners

Made in the USA
Monee, IL
08 September 2021